it could have been so easy

contents

foreward	*vi*
voices	*1*
seasons will shift on their own	*2*
grown man sentiments	*3*
sauvage by dior	*4*
oh, the duality of coffee	*5*
that sunset from ten years ago	*6*
we could have been a team	*7*
a thousand miles	*9*
growing pains	*10*
butterflies	*12*
candy (revisited)	*14*
love is like an egg	*15*
meeting her for the first time	*16*
am i a poet or do i just write sometimes	*19*
8.3.2020 4:20 a.m.	*20*
signs	*21*
like an old friend	*22*
cop-out	*23*
limelight	*24*
another story on being black in amerika	*26*
land of the free	*27*
these empty tears i cry	*28*
class clown	*29*
how to hate	*30*
on our government doing dumb shit	*31*
the concept of nothing // ouroboros	*32*
the renaissance (the indefinite work in progress)	*33*
lots of love	*35*
why he plays video games	*36*
revelations	*37*
revelations (2020)	*38*
carefree/weightless	*40*
woes of a writer	*41*

foreward

    i can't help but be slightly disappointed with myself that it's taken me this long to publish a collection. i decided that i would self publish years ago in 2016. it feels like as soon as i decided to do this, to attempt to create a decently sized collection, writing became ten times more difficult.

    i started to experience writers' block like i've never dealt with before. i struggled to write anything i felt confident about, and i frequently put off writing as something i just couldn't do at the time. i think i may have just been terrified out of my mind.

    even as i write this, and finalize the pieces that will be in this collection, i can't help but be shook. i've always wanted to make poetry more accessible to people, i've always wanted to help people enjoy something that i find so much love and passion in. but just like any other creative out there, i can't ignore the itch deep in my soul that's screaming at me to stop what i'm doing and keep my work to myself. rejection is real, and rejection of your art hurts you in a way no person could come close to.

    i'm sure others can relate, but when you create, you invest a portion of your most vulnerable self into that creation. it's an extension of you, crude and rough as it may be. no matter how much you try to play it off like you'll be fine whether it's received well or not, there's always that voice holding you back, and telling you to stop where you are. that voice is not letting up on me. it's taking all of me not to ball this up right now.

    you know when miles is holding peter over the dimension portal-thing in *into the spiderverse* and they talk about how you have to take that "leap of faith" into the unknown? i'm peter in that scene. that's kind of how i feel right now. fear of messing up, of flopping, making something that's absolutely terrible, has been holding me back for years. i'm not saying that i've gotten it all figured out now or that i no longer am thinking about how this will be received. i guess at this point i don't care as much as i previously did, and maybe that's a good thing.

so, here i am, taking this leap of faith.

i waited so long to grow up only to end up wanting to be a kid again. i just want to wake up to a full breakfast, play outside all day, video games all night, rinse, and repeat. things were just so much easier, before we all got older. before we started seeing life through a different lens, or having responsibilities and commitments. i remember a sweet happiness day in and day out, that youthful naivety that is so precious, it's heartbreaking knowing how finite it truly is.

voices

i remember the days
where we would laugh and play
in the middle of august.
those days where the sun
had no bounds. we played

until we couldn't breathe, until
our voices were no more than
shallow sounds lost in the breeze
that carried them until they
lost meaning.

looking back, i wonder when that day came.
when did those voices fall mute?
at what point did they fade away?

or maybe, are they out there?
still floating on the wind,
lofty clouds that will never rain?

seasons will shift on their own

we're not kids anymore, and it's bittersweet.
we've changed. i'm not bitter, i pray you're not.

along the way, we forget that we have to grow up,
and grow apart.
my mother told me life is ever changing seasons,
winter isn't spring, and fall isn't summer.

is it not foolish to wear a fur in the rain,
or a swimsuit in the snow?

seasons will shift on their own,
and we are nothing but clouds.
it is not so wrong to assume
we were only passing through.

grown man sentiments

i got a pair of starburys when i was ten.
didn't want them,
i actually wanted some heelys instead.
wanted to be like my friends
and trip over pebbles
and get tucked into bed with band-aids.
my mom told me to stop focusing on their plates and look
at mine.

i had a fork, spoon, and knives,
grown man portions: eyes the size of my stomach.
she was right —
i never liked training wheels, or cheat codes,
or elbow pads or nightlights.
grown men aren't scared to fall,
so why am i?
why am i twenty years old shopping on the heelys web-
site?

sauvage by dior

paid my mom a visit.
i think she's a tad depressed
i smell like a man.

oh, the duality of coffee

i brew my coffee how my mom likes it.
just a little sugar,
and just a little cream,
kind of bitter, but also a little sweet.

each sip's a shot of her voice,
shouting up the stairs
in the mornings before school.

i was running late,
she had already called my name three times
as her coffee cooled.

by the time i came down,
she was heated,
her coffee was cold.

nowadays, nothing has changed.
i run late as often as the sun rises,
every morning a race through the front door.

as i hurry and down my mug i can hear her,
making sure i'm up, that i haven't lost my way.

that sunset from ten years ago

there was something about that memory of that sunset
from ten years ago,
with the summer cold closing in on my parent's old bones
and the summer bliss embracing my naive young kiss...
i just want to go back sometimes.
sometimes, i miss the lights, sights, frights,
the bruises, blood, and peroxide,
young minds sanctified by pure fun outside.

i remember playing roller hockey in the street
but i got grounded for throwing the puck at some teeth.
nobody got hurt, and the next day
we were back at it, finding random exotic leaves.
it was fun.

i remember playing video games
when it was raining outside
and fighting over who got to be player one.
now i remember when
there were perfect clouds in the sky
and we were playing video games
until the stories were done.
that was yesterday.

we could have been a team

you just turned twenty-one,
and i just forgot,
for the fourth year
...in a row.

when we were younger,
maybe twelve and ten,
or ten and eight,
remember that school bus?

we were running late,
running to catch the bus.
i was bigger than you, and so,
i was faster.

(you swear that you were just as fast as me,
yet every time we raced, you came in last)

mrs. kurtz, the bus driver,
curse her soul, damn her,
never waited an extra second!
not for you, not for me.

now, i'll be honest,
at the time, on my mind,
all i could see
was a seat on that bus.

you couldn't keep up with me,
and you're not to blame.
you tripped, you fell. it happens.

i only barely heard you,
and i regret it still today,
because ever since that day,
you have never called out for me.

i think about that day a lot.
every time i see you,
i see you from that day.
i wonder, if things were different,

if when you had called out to me
i turned around and helped you up
and we got to school as a team,
would we be a team today?

if just one day was different,
could i just forget it,
and remember something else,
like your birthday, for once?

a thousand miles

did you ever think we'd get here?
riding through the sounds, windows down,
not a thought in mind,
losing our minds,
losing the chance to be true to ourselves,
losing the chance to ask why we're here in the first place,

why we even drove this far when gas is that expensive,
because it wasn't for the view (which isn't bad.)

the sun is setting down the road, it's lighting the way,
we'll be home way after the street lights come on — wait,
we're way too far from home to think about street lights,
yet the way the sunset blinks off the trees,
it seems like we never left.

the road's been paved, it's smooth and black,
not a bump present, but i swear we hit a pothole or two.
three hours on the same road, playlist set to loop,
i know your favorite album word for word.

we only just got here,
i'm still taking it all in,
i'm still trying to think why we drove here just for this,
all the pit stops and rest areas,
the diners at 5 a.m.,

for a goal, we didn't achieve much,
just some milage and some memories.
was that your goal?
these memories?

growing pains

i've been waiting to be a kid again
ever since i turned twenty.
and if i could talk to myself when i was sixteen
i'd say to take heed of the warnings.

it all does fly by, and i wasn't ready for the wind
my hat flew off and i got off balanced
now i'm just doing what i can
to not get swept up in it

it's not a tornado, yet, it has potential yet,
it's too bad i don't have an emergency plan set.
it's enough to brave the storm in front of me,
fighting for a chance just to brave the next.

if i would have red the signs,
the fine print between the lines,
i'd be more equipped to handle this,
but i haven't met one who has.

(although i'd love to)

i think about those days quite a bit. it seems like these days there's just always something. i don't remember a day in the past few years that i wasn't worrying about something, or plainly stressed about what i had yet to finish. these days, there's always something to be stressed about. it all was so easy back then, everything was so simple.

butterflies

allow me to introduce myself
i mean, is that okay with you?
i didn't mean to interrupt
or come across as abrupt
but i'm so used to seeing in black and white
and you're emulating such a bright light —
i can't help myself
i'm noah
(damnit, I said my name wrong)

                hey
           i just, uh
            (think!)
          what's up
            ?wait!
           where—
           o-okay
        see you later
      —are you going?

(how do you smell?)
i think pretty good, i mean —
(too much cologne)
hope not, hope she doesn't
(your jeans are too tight)
my jeans are fine,
oh, hey! hi
(you're too awkward)
(just talk to her)
...well, that was superb.

(you will say something today!)
yeah, that isn't stupid
or maybe she thinks it's cute
when i fumble over my lines
(you're losing time just say something!)
hey, how are y—
(too generic)
the weather's nic—
(it's raining, stupid!)
i-
(you're fumbling)
but,
she laughed?
(giggled)

do you mind if we start over?
the way i freeze up,
it's not a habit. i usually play it
cool as a cooler,
but with you,
i can't move
as smooth as i mean to.
if we could start from the top,
i'd love to learn your name.
i'm noah, and you are?

candy (revisited)

you remind me of a song
that i never knew i'd sing,
and you make me think of sweets—
candies we'd eat as kids
that taste a little too sweet now,

but even now,
if you were to make them,
i think i would ask you,

my love, how many times has someone said,
the way you make these, you could make the sun dance,
way before its turn to shine?

with your eyes, and your smile,
you remind me of a dance i'd never move to,
unless it was you pulling my hand.

i'm a kid in a candy store,
and you're making sweets
that take me back
to when we were free.

and everything i want to say
will never leave my tongue,

yet i know you'd convince me,
to let go and taste the sweets.

to be free once again,
something too sweet to be natural.
something artificial,
something like candy.

love is like an egg

love is like an egg
that you're balancing on a spoon
but the spoon is upside down
and you're standing on a waterbed.

meeting her for the first time

his breath left him in that moment.
he had never imagined meeting one as lovely,
a beauty so warm,
winters could be bearable in her company.

her eyes, a brown like chocolate,
sweet and delicate,
a smile that interrupts the room,
the sun flirting with her skin.
she was glowing.

he just wanted to know her name,
her story, from start to finish,
he wanted every detail,
he wanted to know her.

she was a riddle,
and he wanted to figure her out.

love is a beautiful thing, isn't it? it's crazy how something as pure and powerful as love is so closely related to the fragility of hate. it's almost as if they're two sides of the same coin, and the emotions can be decided with a single coin flip.

sometimes i wonder if i'm doing this correctly. if i'm living right. they always say to live like it's your last day, to go balls to the wall, and make some great memories along the way. looking back i've missed out on so many great memories. memories that i regret not having to this day.

that being said, i don't think that i can live like i'll be dead tomorrow. i just don't think that's in me. but it's not very fun to live for the distant future either.

i don't think it'd be a bad idea to live like i will wake up tomorrow, right?

am i a poet or do i just write sometimes

i pick up and put the pen down so many times
it's clear to me i'm just trying to be someone i'm not.
i'm supposed to be a poet!
i'm supposed to have words wrapped around my pinky,
and notebooks filled with pieces i'll never finish,
but instead i have three
from three different eras
and not a single one is more than a quarter full.

shouldn't i feel like i can write my way through my head?
like a quick haiku or two is nothing for me?
i heard that i should set hours aside to write
and all i could do was wonder why would
someone have that much to say,
or why anyone would want to read all that.

i used to think poets caught lightning in bottles
and now i think they just put some notes in them
and toss them out to sea,
and hopefully one day someone will pick it up
and enjoy what they read, even if it's just one person.

if one person happens to enjoy my ramblings,
i like to think i'd be satisfied.

8.3.2020 4:20 a.m.

all that i can feel is envy.
i see my peers and the art they create
and i so desperately want to be them.

i look at my years upon years
of unfinished projects,
and stories i'm still figuring out,

and look at them with their
neatly packaged masterpiece,
acting like i can't see the failures behind it.

the nights of doubt, days of worry,
that voice saying their work is worthless,
the same voice i'm listening to right now.

one day, if i finish my own creation,
i'll make sure to read this over,
so i don't act like it came out of thin air.

that day, i'll remind myself of this night,
when i felt like putting the pen down,
once and for all,

just so i can tell myself,
every moment leading up to this
was 100% worth it.

signs

why am i so mad all the time?
i really don't know why
i'm in my bed and i can't sleep
for the fifth night in a row!
maybe it's a sign,
a sign that i can't read,
telling me that maybe
i've been doing this all wrong
for quite a while.
maybe i'm full of maybes
'cause i'm always unsure
about the next day, and the day after that,
and i'm so mad from driving in fog
for as long as i've had gas.
maybe the weather will clear up soon.
i hope it does, because i'm falling behind,
and soon i might as well pull over
or turn around and head back

like an old friend

i hate mirrors. i'm not photogenic.
the one that looks back,
the one that meets my gaze,

smells of cigarettes, eyes that almost scream with con-
tempt,
conceit crawling from his clothes, like beggars
for quarters from the shade of the street corner,
slick black two-piece, oxfords to match,
asking, almost laughing, why i don't come to visit anymore.

asking why i don't answer his calls.
he knows he's not blocked, he knows.
he asks this, with a grin, because he knows,
sooner or later, i'll have to open my door,
like an old friend.

me, personally, i'm dreading that day.

cop-out

it's okay to make mistakes
but i'm running out of time
and i got two strikes
and new doubts —

do i even like the crowd?
it's getting a little too loud,
at this rate, i'll likely freeze up,
or act out, and look like a clown.

what i could do is swing like the greats,
i can imitate the same patterns,
i can fall in line and still be remembered,
i can just take the road more travelled.

limelight

i'm scared of so much shit,
i'm scared to go to bars,
ever since i crashed,
i'm kind of scared of cars,

i'm scared of too much attention,
but i want to be an icon.
it's like i want the spotlight
two steps to the right of me.

sometimes, i try to imagine living life like i'm not a black man and i realize it's literally impossible for me to do so. all my life, the color of my skin has been pivotal to how i was perceived by others. i've made a fool of myself and let myself be ridiculed, and for a long time, truly hated that i looked different from my peers. i felt alienated, and could not find anything about me that i loved. it wasn't until i got older that i found self love and began to love being black. although i'd like to assume i'm the only one that dealt with this kind of self hate, i'm sure plenty of other people who look just like me went through similar trials as they grew up. it'd be easy to say all of it was for a purpose, but i don't think it was. sometimes that's just the way things are, as unfair as it is.

however, despite all that, we're still here, and we love ourselves now. i hope that love for ourselves keeps us going in our darkest moments.

another story on being black in amerika

how many times can i cry about the same story?
i think i've lost count,
yet my tears no longer have meaning.

they carry the weight of a hollowed book,
the story of someone already forgotten
with an ending so similar, if you're not careful,
you'd forget whose you're reading.

since when was it okay for these tales to end the same,
i'd ask myself, before i opened a history book.
since when, no,
when was it okay to truly be surprised?
at what point were we stunned by the sunrise?

when did we forget, we were given land
with a slope so steep, you'd be stupid to think
rain wouldn't wash away everything we built
every time our trees got too high.

land of the free

this place has always been a joke to me.
the kind of joke that's not really funny
and you only laugh so the moment passes,
except the moment stays put.

so you're stuck in that moment for, roughly,
two hundred and fifty years, or something.
it gets to a point where the joke is lame,
or it just was never funny at all.

i guess i should ask then.
what's the point of a joke
that's about as funny
as a stinking sack of shit?

these empty tears i cry

i've tried so many times to write this.
i have tried so many times to put into words,
to paint some sort of crude portrait
of these empty tears i cry.

i'm long past the point
of another dead black boy
meaning anything to me.

i will look at his face
those dirt colored cheeks, those eyes like almonds,
with an innocence not much different than mine.

eyes that will never see these words,
ears that will never hear love again,
a soul that will never know the newest trends.

these tears i cry used to fall like bricks,
now, they float like feathers,
they linger and lurk, telling a cruel joke,
that maybe april fools day made a mistake
and fell on august instead of april.

maybe none of this is true,
maybe that black boy woke up,
maybe, just maybe, his face felt warm again.

maybe i like to lie to myself, and say it's fake,
so i don't have to face my fears.
maybe he will wake up.
maybe, i mean, maybe,
a black boy can dream?

class clown

my ashy skin was always different from my friends.
i could draw pictures on it.

they'd appear as bright white gashes on my forearm.
i'd get home and receive a scolding from mom:

"since when did i allow you to leave the house
lookin like a damned fool?!"

well, screw you mom,
my friends think I'm the coolest around.

how to hate

i would go inside at high noon
when the sun was at its peak
out of fear of getting darker.

i never wanted to be told
that i was black as the room
once the lights were off,

or black as the shirt i wore,
so black, you couldn't tell
whether or not i was in the nude.

i was afraid of the word black.

i feared that the blacker i became
the less friends i would make.
i wish i found love for myself
before i learned how to hate.
maybe then i could have had
some nice memories of the sun.

on our government doing dumb shit

i thought this river
had run dry a week ago.
still, i'm not surprised.

the concept of nothing // ouroboros

i don't think we're supposed to understand
what it means not to be.
i don't think i can conceptualize
the absence of what makes me...me.
what does it mean to skate without the pavement,
or to paint without a canvas?

i find myself thinking about not thinking about
thinking about the absence of thought
in order to think about what i thought was an idea of null.
maybe what i thought was transparent
might be more opaque
and maybe the liberties i take
might be the root of my mistakes.

if we were bigger than this life,
we could spend more time weighing the odds
about what existed before nothing did
and what exactly nothing is.
i think i'd like to think
nothing and something are two sides of a coin,
or a snake eating its tail.

the renaissance (the indefinite work in progress)

so there i was, and there you were, all of us,
everyone, dangling their feet off the rooftop.
four distinctly different artists caught in the same painting
yet, none of us holding the paintbrush to our passions,
yet.

ambitious, yes, focused, not so much, motivated?
most definitely.

dedicated to manipulation,
to making a masterpiece for the masses,
a decision to "form a more perfect union".
to map a new demographic before our deaths.

if our desire was to make a mark, well,
we'd be done already.
the mark's been made, but not engraved,
and for it to stay we need to stomp on it
until our own foot decays.

and these days, most pictures will fade,
so as us four sat there, dancing with the devil,
we dared to begin drafting on our canvas.
with no brush, but our own fingers,
our own blood, sweat, tears, and elbow grease,
finally finding the paintbrush to be figurative,
that we were manipulated ourselves.

we learned to picture the paintbrush as our pointer,
our palms the palettes, our pinkies the varnish,
a promise our piece would never be vandalized.

the world is your oyster, they say,
and the city was our canvas,
where we painted nothing but pearls,
rare commodities for the communities to cherish
until our masterpiece,
the indefinite work in progress, is completed.

lots of love

i've only shown my parents my writing once
for a poetry contest that sent me to vegas.
i never really appreciated the empty "ooo's" and "ahh's"
that they always gave me.
not the gleeful squeals they gave to my little brother
when he wrote a "my role model" paper on the church
pastor,
or the wide grin and printed pages when my older sister
wrote a fashion article about crop tops.
i just recently upgraded to thumbs up emojis though,
so maybe I'll show my mom the cover page.

but please,
if my mom ever reads these,
tell her that "lol" does not mean
lots of love.

why he plays video games

everyone knew, including him,
that if you sat too close to the screen,
your eyes would die.
but nobody knew, but him,
that if you sit too far away,
you miss out on the experience.
it's why he plays!

revelations

if i were to talk to god,
i imagine that he would look like an aging french artist
living in germany,
with a slightly severe case of depression
and also an unsettling smoking addiction.

i imagine he would be living in an apartment room barely
big enough for his ego.
with nothing but a bed and a nightstand
with an ash tray and a bottle of whiskey, half full.
and between puffs of smoke he would sip from a lowball
glass, and sit.

he'd keep his door unlocked, for no one ever visits,
and when they do, they assume they've opened the wrong
door
and they would quickly go search for the man they
thought he was.
he'd let out a chuckle between sips.

however, if i were to meet this artist,
i would just ask him what he's done.
and he will reply, with smoke trailing from his nostrils and
the tone of a drunk,
"hell if I know."

revelations (2020)

it's not like i didn't want to come by,
i couldn't find your room.
maybe i didn't recognize you,
you got the face of someone i can tell it all to,
and i just don't remember that.

despite the rumors you're very plain,
but it seems as if you prefer it that way.
you don't look as depressed as before,
if anything, you look fairly bored.

although you look different,
although times have changed,
my question remains the same.
i have always wanted to ask you face to face,
what have you done?

you told me that you've done nothing,
that you just mapped out a plan.

i understand that it's not always your decision,
but i can't ignore this anger
that keeps me from sleeping soundly.
is it laziness or genius that keeps you from
grabbing the reins yourself?

what keeps me so angry is the expectation
that blindly following your advice is the key
to my salvation.
when exactly during my darkest moments
did you prove to me you were worth listening to?

when was i supposed to let go of this rage?

it's that madness that keeps me from
fully accepting what you offer,
but i'm trying to.

maybe i'll carry this with me all my life,
but you got the face of someone who knows
no matter what, it'll be alright.
and i can't explain exactly what,

but i'll try to follow your plan,
because you make me feel
like it's all working out
exactly as it's intended to.

carefree/weightless

sometimes you want to stop time in that one moment of
bliss.
it's the best feeling, isn't it?
when everything couldn't be better, when you're laughing,

and that laugh couldn't be sweeter, more wholesome,
more natural. in that moment,
you were weightless, and carefree.

and that weight, or lack thereof,
it carries you miles, all in that same spot,
not even the greatest forces, not even gravity,

could limit you even for a minute, not for a moment.
these pockets in time,
are these not what we live for?

woes of a writer

a lot of time spent
having miscellaneous conversations with the air.
stupid questions like, "how's your day," acting as if it'd
give an answer,
or a whisper of inspiration, or a confirmation,
that we will create a masterpiece before finding peace
with a piece of our minds
becoming a little less peaceful by the day.
soon our minds will turn into violent catapults hurling out
sentence after sentence making our paper bleed
black, blue, red, grey,
joining a cult created by the letters we created ourselves,
falling into the abyss these stanzas invite us into.
don't get me wrong, it sounds terrible, but it's home.
there's no place like it,
where these words are so much more than words,
they're family.
we get into arguments that erupt into something sinister,
our desks become littered with papers that wilt and wither
into nothing more than liters upon liters
of a liquor that'll tempt us into becoming outspoken
drunkards.
but that's the goal:
to be outspoken.

xxx

at first i didn't really like the name, *it could have been so easy.* i think that it sounds very lazy. when i put this small collection together, i never imagined that i would end up thinking that very statement multiple times a day. if i had just listened when i was younger, if i had just made better decisions, if i had spoken up that one time, or maybe if i had just let loose a little, things could have been different. it could have been so easy to get through life had i just listened.

but i wonder, if it had been easier, if life was a smooth road with no bumps or roundabouts, would i be sitting here writing this now? had everything gone according to plan i don't think i would have turned to the arts as an outlet, and poetry as a passion. every mistake and road block i've encountered has led me to putting this together. and i'm incredibly thankful that my path has led me here, no matter what has happened before now.

it could have been so easy, except that it wasn't. and that's okay.

Made in the USA
Columbia, SC
09 September 2020